501 Writers
Useful Phrases

A selection of 501 short, descriptive phrases, expressions and one liners to give your writing that extra punch along with some 'strong' verbs to give your writing a lift.

QUENTIN COPE

MECURIAN BOOKS

https://mecurianbooks.com

COPYRIGHT & DISCLAIMER

CONTENTS

:Introduction:

:Phrases:

INTRODUCTION

So, what will you do when you get to page 25 and you fall unexpectedly upon that one single sentence; one that simply does not look right; somehow inhibits the pace of a fast flowing chapter and does not describe accurately how your character looked or felt?

You may be one of those fortunate writers who can simply knock the words out, get them down on the page and after a morning of recording a score of 2,000 relax over lunch and a large glass of Chardonnay.

However, you may be one of those poor unfortunates who strive over every sentence, knowing well what you want to write, but reluctantly unable to find the precise little phrase to more exactly attach to the moment.

Competent writing often requires reference to a Dictionary or a Thesaurus. Good writers carry a recording device of some sort around with them or fall back upon that good old fashioned 'pen & paper' to record things they read, see and hear in everyday life. These 'Scribblings' are the sounds, the words and the sights of reality … the 'real' things that people say to one another and the 'real' way they describe things they have seen and events they have witnessed.

With a Dictionary, Thesaurus and Scribblings all

being put to good use, the experienced writer will collect over time a 'Golden Book' … or 'Golden Computer File'. This will contain the condensed results of all the searching and researching for that short, concise 'Golden' sentence.

However you approach your writing projects; whether you find writing hard or easy, most of us will be prepared to admit we can do with all the help available. Of course, if you are one of the 'special ones' who simply need no help at all in your well established and highly profitable writing career, then please put this book down now.

For the rest of us, this little gem contains 501 useful phrases and 'Scribblings' organized in such a way that any writer can quickly navigate to a phrase for use in a particular situation; or one that will remind them of another that will fit the bill nicely.

This is not an answer to a 'writer's prayer', but it is a great second line reference book of phrases you can use every day in your writing journey. So, what does '501 Writers Useful Phrases' contain?

The book is divided in to ten sections and each one contains 50 short phrases, quotes, expressions or complete sentences to fit a particular subject heading.
 The last section contains 51 entries making a total of 501 for this edition. You may find one or two entries appear repetitive but that normally only happens when a particular phrase will fit more than one situation.

Appearance: This section contains some phrases and descriptive lines relating to how a character (looks) looked or (appears) appeared. It contains references to facial expression and the appearance of an individual or place.

Conversation: Here you will find a section of phrases, expressions and observations relating to how characters speak, how a conversation takes place or what has been learnt or surmised from a conversation.

Fear: This is a subject that has many parameters, but you will definitely find some phrases contained within this section to describe the kind of fear experienced by your character or the fear generated by a particular moment in time.

Feelings: This again is a broad subject that attempts to describe feelings in a mix of situations. Feelings of love, belief, disbelief, passion and reflection are provided to set the mood of a particular moment through the eyes of your character.

Opinion: This is a section covering the subject of opinion, which is simply that ... Opinion! Most of the phrases in this section relate to one individual's opinion of another … or of a particular situation. One person's opinion of him/herself may differ from the opinion held by others.

Philosophical: There are a stack of useful quotes here covering a variety of subjects. This section is worth a regular visit as even if a particular phrase does not fit your pre-constructed scenario, there may be some that will trigger a useful line of thought.

Senses: This section provides a few useful lines relating to how a character senses situations or gains an impression of a scenario. Once again, this is a broad subject and it's impossible to summarize how the senses of a character lead him or her through a particular situation, but hopefully you will find some good links or triggers here.

Tenacity: This section describes situations and examples of tenacity taken or seen from your characters viewpoint, or that of others. One person's idea of tenaciousness will again differ greatly from another, but there are 50 very useful entries here to work with.

Time: Here are a few phrases and descriptions of 'time' as seen by a character or as seen in a particular and relative setting. Of course, we all know that 'Tempus Fugit'… but how do you describe it? There are entries here that will relate directly to time or to timelessness and there are 50 to choose from.

Viewpoints: Everyone has a different view of a similar situation and this section provides a broad listing of views and viewpoints relating to people and situations. This section is similar in subject matter to 'Appearance' but concentrates much more on a particular viewpoint relating to the appearance of an individual, group or scenario.

Hopefully, you the reader ... and more importantly, you the writer, will gain something from this writer's phrasebook. As this is a new edition we have added a section relating to the sticky subject of 'Verbs' and as the understanding and use of 'strong' verbs seems to be an issue affecting every writer, hopefully you will take the subject on-board and prosper because of it.

By the way, please don't take it all too seriously ... writing is meant to be fun!

Part 1:
All About Verbs

STRONG VERBS THAT WILL GIVE YOUR WRITING A LIFT

Why do some parts of your writing look alive and vibrant ... and other parts appear dull and unexciting? Have you ever asked yourself that question? Kicking the adverbs and adjectives into touch when you were told as a child these grammatical 'knights of the road' were to be admired and encouraged in a young writer's work.

'I believe the road to hell is paved with adverbs, and I will shout it from the rooftops.' This is a famous quote from that author of authors, Stephen King.

Many proof readers and editors would probably agree that we should aim to write using nouns and verbs and not adjectives and adverbs. The mantra for many would be, when unsure ... remove it! We are all pretty well computerized now, but in the 'good old days' when the 'blue pencil' reigned supreme, editors could be pretty ruthless with more than a third of every page blanked out with the infamous blue marker. Now, in the twenty-first century, we might say that verbs are good, but strong verbs are better.

So, how do we really know what might be regarded as 'strong' verbs? Well, here is a list of verbs we understand to be 'passive' rather than vibrant or strong and once you recognize what they are, the picture will become clearer.

PASSIVE VERBS: Is, Am, Are, Was, Were, Be, Being, Been, Have, Has, Had, Do, Does, Did, Shall, Will, Should, Would, May, Might, Must, Can, Could

Are we suggesting you should never use these verbs? No we are not. Evaluating their use in a sentence is however an essential part of any editing process so here are a few common examples we have found for you to look out for.

EXAMPLES:

Passive: Roger was walking down the road.
Strong: Roger **strode** down the road.

Passive: Gemma likes living in the country.
Strong: Gemma **treasures** country living.

Passive: There are three things that make me feel like this …
Strong: Three things **convince** me…

OK. Now we can recognize the bad guys, it would be useful to have some sort of list of strong verbs for comparison. So, here is a list of 198 Strong Verbs for you to consider when you next embark on a novel writing or editing exercise.

A LIST OF STRONG VERB EXAMPLES (198)
Absorb, Advance, Advise, Alter, Amend, Amplify, Attack

Balloon, Bash, Batter, Beam, Beef, Blab, Blast, Bolt, Boost, Brief, Broadcast, Brood, Burst

Capture, Catch, Charge, Chap, Chip, Clasp, Climb, Clutch, Collide, Command, Cower

Dangle, Dash, Demolish, Depart, Deposit, Detect, Deviate, Devour, Direct, Discern, Discover

Eavesdrop, Engage, Engulf, Enlarge, Ensnare, Envelop, Erase, Escort, Expand, Explore

Fight, Fish, Fling, Fly, Frown, Fuse, Garble, Gaze, Glare, Gleam, Glisten, Glitter, Gobble

Hack, Hail, Heighten, Hobble, Hover, Hurry, Ignite, Illuminate, Inspect, Instruct, Intensify

Jostle, Journey, Lash, Launch, Lead, Leap, Locate, Lurch, Lurk

Magnify, Mimic, Mint, Moan, Modify, Multiply, Muse, Mushroom, Mystify

Notice, Notify

Obtain, Oppress, Order

Paint, Park, Peck, Peek, Peer, Perceive, Picture, Pilot, Pinpoint, Place, Plant, Plop, Plunge

Realize, Recite, Recoil, Refashion, Refine, Remove, Report, Retreat, Reveal, Reverberate

Saunter, Scamper, Scan, Scorch, Scrape, Scratch, Scrawl, Seize, Serve, Shatter, Shepherd

Shimmer, Shine, Shock, Shrivel, Sizzle, Skip, Skulk, Slash, Slide, Slink, Slip, Slump, Slurp

Smash, Smite, Snag, Snarl, Sneak, Snowball, Soar, Spam, Sparkle, Sport, Sprinkle, Stare

Starve, Steal, Steer, Storm, Strain, Stretch, Strip, Stroll, Struggle, Stumble, Supercharge

Tail, Tattle, Toddle, Transfigure, Transform, Travel, Treat, Trim, Trip, Trudge, Tussle

Uncover, Unearth, Untangle, Unveil, Usher

Veil,

Wail, Weave, Wind, Withdraw, Wreck, Wrench, Wrest, Wrestle, Wring, Yank
Zing, Zap

Part 2:
Appearance

This section provides some phrases and descriptive lines relating to how a character (looks) looked or (appears) appeared. It contains references to facial expression and the appearance of an individual or place.

01: He had a face like a bulldog chewing a wasp.

02: He/she beheld a face sunken beyond pain.

03: The hard smile appeared frozen in the beam of the barrier lights.

04: He/she took on a look of anticipation.

05:He/she gave out a look that would quicken any pulse.

06: It was a menacing look, full of authority.

07: It appeared a frightening pallor of deathly white.

08: He gave out his best panty-dropping grin.

09: He/she appeared as a person of flushed porcine features.

10: He was dripping, his clothes permanently damp in what could only be described as a Sauna-like climate.

11: He/she was convinced that would put a 'smile on her/his dial'.

12: It was a smile that nearly became laughter.

13: Appearing before him came a terrifying specter.

14: The appearance was that of a watery shimmer.

15: He/she gazed in her/his direction with critical eyes.

16: The eyes were alert and intelligent.

17: The eyes appeared reduced to sharp points, ready to pierce any lies.

18: The eyes revealed a certain shrewdness.

19: The eyes told no story, staring through and beyond.

20: His/her face tightened like a mask.

21: He/she appeared far too impressed with himself/herself.

22: He/she stood trapped in the sight line of glacial blue eyes.

23: He/she appeared to have bookended a certain era.

24: He/she looked as if he had received a promise from a liar.

25: He/she gradually took on a sanguine expression.

26: He/she arrived in the room; tall and moving gracefully.

27: His/her eyes glazed over like a crazed windscreen.

28: It was in his/her eyes; a sign of intensity.

29: Is there a chin behind the beard she wondered?

30: It was a look luscious with promise.

31: It was perspiration like a hot shower.

32: She appeared austere but with a haughty manner.

33: He/she was either confident, or had left the gas on.

34: There was something in the eyes making you want to look away.

35: He/she appeared to be somewhere between twenty one and dead.

36: He/she held a stony expression.

37: He/she turned; the eyes had lost their friendliness.

38: She was all over him like a rash.

39: He was all over her like a cheap suit.

40: here was the disguise of delicacy in her look.

41: He appeared unwelcome to the point of being 'persona non grata'.

42: A certain bitterness crept into his/her face.

43: He possessed a charming air of vigor and vitality.

44: He/she displayed a curious and inexplicable uneasiness.

45: He enjoyed a dandified, pretty-boy looking sort of figure.

46: He/she looked a disheveled and distraught figure.

47:.A faint, transient, wistful smile lightened his/her brooding face.

48:.The figure was captured beneath the cold glare of the desolate night.

49:.He/she appeared to be buried in the quick sands of ignorance.

50:.The eyes were dull black under the precipice of brows.

Part 3:
Conversation

Here you will find a section of phrases and observations relating to how characters speak, how a conversation takes place or what has been learnt or surmised from a conversation.

51: It was a short conversation, followed by a Hollywood pause.

52: He/she knew immediately, it was a poor choice of words.

53: It was a post-ironic answer.

54: Although what he says is responsible, he does not want to be responsible for saying it!

55: He/she spoke with an accent like warm honey.

56: He/she had an attractive voice.

57: He/she spoke with a cut glass accent.

58: In the world of conversation, he/she was still developing his/her techniques.

59: 'Can you more clearly define your question' he asked archly?

60: He/she could charm a tortoise out of a shell.

61: He/she could talk his/her way out of a room with no doors.

62: It felt like the word 'hope' climbed out of

the dictionary, packed its bags and walked away.

63: It was obvious by the conversation that patience had deserted him.

64: She said his name as if holding it with tongs.

65: The conversation was interrupted by the soundtrack of everyday life.

66: The words packed an unwelcome (unexpected) punch.

67: He/she used words weighted with emotion.

68: And yet the explanation did not wholly satisfy him/her.

69: She knew instantly he was open to persuasion.

70: Did he presume too much in the conversation?

71: Did he/she think there was anything ominous in the saying of it?

72: No matter what was being said, he knew that everyone would look at it differently.

73: Forgive me if I seem disobliging in my conversation.

74: From his conversation, his sense of humor was unquenchable.

75: However, she would have liked to hear his views.

76: I always welcome criticism so long as it is sincere.

77: He/she was curious to learn what his/her motives were.

78: He/she confessed to being a little discouraged.

79: He/she confessed it was not at all in the secret of his/her ambitions.

80: He/she was not capable of unraveling the conversation.

81: He/she was not going into sordid details.

82: He/she was not going to pay him/her any idle compliments.

83: He/she had been persuaded by his/her candor.

84: She knew he was suppressing many of the details.

85: She was sure he could pay her no higher compliment.

86: She was grateful, in fact very much flattered.

87: He was wondering if he may dare ask her a personal question.

88: She could easily understand his undisguised astonishment.

89: He could not altogether acquit himself of interested motives.

90: After such a conversation, I dare say your intuition could be right.

91: He did not doubt the sincerity of her arguments.

92: He stated how deeply indebted he felt for their kindness.

93: May I venture to ask what inference you would draw from that.

94: She knew from the tone of the conversation, his attitude would be one of disapproval.

95: Now he knew she was being flippant.

96: Whatever was being said, he didn't want to press her against her will.

97: Please do not think I am asking out of mere curiosity.

98: She/he was carefully and purposely reading between the lines.

99: She had an extraordinary gift of conversation.

100: He/she wanted to be shown that the two cases were analogous.

Part 4:
Fear

This is a subject that has many parameters, but you will definitely find some phrases contained within this section to describe the kind of fear experienced by your character.

101: A cold hand closed around his/her heart.

102: It had become a pulse pounding event.

103: The strong smell of fear was present in the room.

104: If he cut of all his/her demons, his/her angels might die too.

105: Death hung in the air like a suffocating blanket.

106: It was fear, not visible to the eye but sharply felt in the heart.

107: He knew his fear as the menace that lurks in the path of life.

109: He/she was left feeling like a lost lamb in an abattoir.

110: His/her heart was going like a stolen moped.

111: In her fear, she knew he would give her nothing, but take from her everything.

112: She was left with panic welling up inside her, a blender of emotions.

113: He/she stood paralyzed by fear.

114: Being fearful, sometimes you have to go towards the thing that makes you want to run away.

115: In his fear, sweat poured in warm rivulets down his face.

116: Be in no doubt, I can make the sun set upon your world and you will no longer cast a shadow in it.

117: In the fear of the moment, time stands still and yet it races.

118: A foreboding of some destined change.

119: A frigid touch of the hand.

120: A ghastly whiteness overspread the cheek.

121: A glassy stare of deprecating horror.

122: A grim and shuddering fascination.

123: A haunting and horrible sense of insecurity.

124: A hint of death in the icy breath of the gale.

125: A new trouble was dawning on his/her thickening mental horizon.

126: A new, uncomfortable perplexity began to invade her/him.

127: A quiver of resistance ran through her/him.

128: A sense of desolation and disillusionment overwhelmed him/her.

129: A shiver of apprehension crisped his/her skin.

130: A somber and breathless calm hung over the deepening eve.

131: A stifling sensation of pain and suspense overcame him/her.

132: She/he knew a thousand unutterable fears would bear irresistible despotism over her confused thoughts.

133: There was a tragic futility in his/her actions.

134: He/she was left agitated with violent and contending emotions

135: In his fear, all the frightening unknown of the night and of the universe pressed upon him/her.

136: He/she noticed an acute note of distress in her voice.

137: She/he felt the iciness, a sinking and sickening of the heart.

138: It was an immediate and obscure thrill of alarm.

139: An uncomfortable premonition of fear swept over him/her.

140: His/her fear went beyond the farthest edge of night.

141: He/she was fearful as drowsiness coiled insidiously about him/her

142: Events took an unexpected and sinister turn.

143: Fear held him in a vice.

144: In the darkness came fleeting touches of something alien and intrusive.

145: In his/her fear, he/she gathered all his/her scattered impulses into one single passionate act of courage.

146: Great shuddering seized on her/him.

147: He/she was haunted with a chill and unearthly foreboding

148: As he stood before her, he made a fearful, loathsome object.

149: He/she perceived the iron hand within the velvet glove.

150: Her/his heart pounded in her/his throat

Part 5:
Feelings

This is a broad subject attempting to describe feelings in a mix of situations. Feelings of love, belief, disbelief, passion and reflection are described to set the mood of any particular moment through the eyes of your character.

151: A bewildering sense of disbelief swept over her.

152: He generated a cocktail of emotions within her.

153: He/she felt it was a 'hurry up and wait' situation.

154: He/she perceived it was a light bulb moment.

155: It was a tense, near religious experience.

156: A tidal wave of hope/despair swept over him/her.

157: He/she felt they had been left in an unnerving situation.

158: The feeling was all thorns and no petals.

159: She/he felt it was a beautiful irony.

160: She/he felt that big definitely is better.

161: He/she felt bone bitingly cold.

162: She had a feeling it was akin to derailing the locomotive of young love

163: He/she felt he/she was drawing comfort in his/her faith.

164: He/she was being taken to ecstasy on a new scale.

165: He/she felt the electric sensations.

166: Every muscle fibre/fiber, every sinew became alive.

167: He/she felt there was some wiggle room in the plan.

168: It was a heart racing, heart stopping, heart breaking feeling.

169: He/she felt that hell is too good for such a piece of garbage.

170: He/she felt there were holes in his/her tapestry.

171: In this situation, she felt that home is where the hugs are.

172: He felt he needed to ask the question 'I can rest when I die then?'

173: He/she liked to travel light and loyalty did not fit in to the overhead bins.

174: If you are not rich, make sure you feel rich. If you can't feel rich then you're dead.

175: I'll hold a good thought for you if you feel it necessary.

176: I feel as if I need you like the desert needs rain.

177: I've felt he was never between us but somehow always in the middle.

178: He/she would feel out of his/her depth in a puddle.

179: He/she had a feeling of quivering inside.

180: He/she felt relief like the passing of a gargantuan stool.

181: He felt it to be no safer than shaving with a flame thrower.

182: He/she could feel it slipping through his/her fingers like mercury.

183: That feeling in the pit of your stomach when you see him/her.

184: He/she felt just about the drunk side of sober.

185: He/she could feel the mood music of the situation was changing.

186: There was a feeling, heightened by the strange mournful mutter of the battlefield.

187: He/she felt they would now have to throw out their heart ahead of them and then chase after it.

188: It felt as if it was such a confused mass of impressions it could be likened to an old rubbish heap.

189: She had a feeling he was a callous and conscienceless brute.

190: He/she was feeling his/her way through a constant stream of rhythmic memories.

191: There followed what felt like a great process of searching and shifting.

192: She/he felt a hot up-rush of hatred and loathing toward him/her.

193: He/she was consumed by a profound and eager hopefulness.

194: She/he was feeling a shuffling compromise between defiance and prostration.

195: He/she felt the soft suspicion of ulterior motives.

196: It was a feeling triggered unexpectedly by a tumultuous rush of sensations.

197: He/she felt completely absorbed in a stream of thoughts and reminiscences.

198: He/she was feeling beset by agreeable hallucinations.

199: She/he felt the whole conversation to be clothed with the witchery of fiction.

200: She/he felt her dreams and visions had been surpassed.

Part 6:
Opinion

This is a section covering the subject of opinion, which is simply that ... Opinion! Most of the phrases in this section relate to one individual's opinion of another … or of a particular situation.

201: A man wants to be a woman's first love; a woman wants to be his last.
202: In his/her opinion, it was turning into a Monty Python moment.
203: His/her opinion was it is better to live one year as a tiger than one hundred as a sheep.
204: The opinion was it is better to travel in expectation than arrive in disappointment.
205: It was purely an opinion as to the cost and benefits of a relationship.
206: In his/her opinion he couldn't sell a black cat to a witch.
207: Do not believe everything you have heard about me, the truth is probably much worse.
208: It's only an opinion, but editing is like cleaning up after a baby, not fun but necessary.
209: Everyone pretends they're something they're not to get to the place they want to be.
210: He had a high opinion of his own talents.
211: It was just an opinion, but he/she could

almost believe this was a good idea.

212: It's only an opinion and I don't know if I loved him. Is that something you would forget?

213: In his/her opinion if brains were tax, he/she should be expecting a rebate.

214: In his/her opinion, if there is one thing worse than being talked about, it's not being talked about.

215: Impossible is merely an opinion.

216: It's a considered opinion that in order to break the code, you need to start by taking into account everything you think you know is wrong.

217: In her opinion, he had a mind like a plain brown envelope.

218: In his opinion, she was nakedly ambitious.

219: He/she was so crooked he/she could hide behind a spiral staircase.

220: It was an opinion cloaked in ten pence psychology.

221: His/her opinion was being delivered through the leaky pipe of ignorance.

222: In her opinion, the only war he ever fought was the inch war.

223: In her opinion, their love was like a rumor, everyone talked about it but no one really knew for sure.

224: His/her contribution was opinionated and as useful as an ashtray on a motorbike.

225: What of the opinion and what thoughts are they that show the alchemy of the mind?

226: It is my opinion that you should never have a clandestine meeting in a clandestine place.

227: It was an opinion contributing to a flood in the affairs of man.

228: It was only an opinion but one that appeared to contain a bewildering labyrinth of facts.

229: In his/her opinion it was a disaster of the first magnitude.

230: He/she offered his/her opinion with a firmness tempered by the most scrupulous courtesy.

231: The opinion offered was simply a flourish of rhetoric.

232: His/her opinion was a haughty self-assertion of equality.

233: From his viewpoint, she displayed a keenly receptive and intensely sensitive temperament.

234: His/her opinion provided a lively sense of what is dishonorable.

235: In her/his opinion, it had the makings of a mercenary marriage.

236: The opinion expressed was simply a

nimble interchange of uninteresting gossip.

237: The opinion offered was purely a patchwork of compromises.

238: The opinion was delivered by a powerful and persuasive orator.

239: There was a sharp difference of opinion.

240: The opinion provided a skeptical suspension of judgment.

241: He/she was opinionated and trapped in a snare of delusion.

242: The verbal delivery turned out to be a somewhat complicated and abstruse calculation.

243: It was only an opinion that had produced such a storm of public indignation.

244: The opinion offered was a strange mixture of carelessness, generosity, and caprice.

245: His/her opinion was delivered in a tone of exaggerated solicitude.

246: His/her opinion seemed based on a whole catalog of disastrous blunders.

247: The opinion was alien to the purpose.

248: It was a brilliant display of ingenious argument.

249: What was being said appeared to be calculated to create disgust.

250: The opinion was one cherishing a huge fallacy.

Part 7:
Philosophical

There are a stack of useful quotes here covering a variety of subjects. This section is worth a regular visit as even if a particular phrase does not fit your pre-constructed scenario, there may be some that will trigger a useful line of thought.

251: A man who has never lost any money, never made any money.

252: A man without fear is a man without hope.

253: A test of leadership is to recognize a problem before it becomes an emergency.

254: Alcohol is the answer, but what is the question.

255: As the purse is emptied, the heart is filled.

256: Bad artists copy, great artists steal.

257: Bad reviews, don't read them, measure them.

258: Before a happy ever after, must come a once upon a time.

259: Blood is thicker than water but a 100 dollar bill is thicker than both.

260: Brevity is the soul of wit (Shakespeare).

261: Coincidences do happen, but they shouldn't happen too often.

262: Courage is one virtue that without the rest is meaningless.

263: Dedication creates order from chaos.

264: Do one thing every day that makes you feel alive.

265: Don't trouble trouble, til trouble troubles you.

266: Essential writing provides essential reading.

267: Every book is the wreck of a once good idea.

268: Failure is trying but not succeeding.

269: Fool me once, shame on you; fool me twice, shame on me.

270: Fools never change their minds and wise men seldom do.

271: Good things take time, great things happen immediately.

272: Good things come to good people.

273: Hating your enemy does not bring him pain.

274: History has a way of delivering the right people in the right place at the right time.

275: If opportunity doesn't knock, you may need to build a door.

276: If things are worth doing, they are worth doing to excess (Oscar Wilde).

277: If you aim for a goal that is not your

destiny, you will always be swimming against the tide.

278: If you are not at the dinner, you are probably not on the menu.

279: If you can imagine it, it can happen.

280: If you can't give them something to love, give them something to hope for.

281: If you have to project, project beyond failure.

282: If you wait by the river long enough, the bodies of your enemies will float by.

283: If you want to change the world, you have to live in it first.

284: Imagination is more important than knowledge (Einstein).

285: Impossible dreams are simply young challenges.

286: In god we trust; all others we monitor.

287: In war, truth is the first casualty.

288: It doesn't matter how many books you get through … It's how many books get through to you.

289: It's a thin line between a blessing and a curse.

290: It's not getting what you want, it's wanting what you get.

291: It's not what is possible but what is probable.

292: Lead, follow or get out of the way.

293: Lessons not learnt in blood are soon forgotten.

294: Life is about getting ahead and staying there.

295: Life is about kicking ass, not licking it.

296: Life is like a sewer, what you get out of it, depends upon what you put in to it.

297: Love is an act of courage.

298: Marriage, a good conversation that got out of hand.

299: Never let the truth spoil a good story.

300: Not being able to know something is no proof that it doesn't exist.

Part 8:
Senses

This section provides a few useful lines relating to how a character senses situations or gains an impression of a scenario.

301: He/she pondered on a cauldron of thoughts.

302: He/she sensed it was a matter of emotional intelligence.

303: The trace of perfume became a pleasant silage.

304: She sensed a red mist moment.

305: He sensed a stratospheric moment.

306: It was a sense of insolent charm.

307: He/she sensed a need to drink and swallow gratefully.

308: He/she sensed a huge, heavy rush suggesting immensity.

309: He sensed some out of the box thinking was required.

310: He sensed it was like a door slamming in his head.

311: Do you have the sense that people seem strange when you're a stranger?

312: He sensed he should set aside his concerns but would not abandon them.

313: It was a long time, in a sense six months without Sundays.

314: The impression was gained, that like a doorknob everyone has had a turn.

315: The smell of the beer laden breath was the smell of freedom.

316: He/she sensed the words had failed, the very language itself unable to convey their proper emotion.

317: She sensed there was no doubting his membership of the Ersatz toffs.

318: Thoughts crowded through his mind.

319: There was a sense of viewing the matter through the telescope of memory.

320: She sensed she could contain the passion in her heart no more than he could control the breath that he took.

321: It seemed a burlesque feint of evading a blow.

322: He sensed a bitterness creeping into her face.

323: It appeared as a cunning intellect patiently diverting every circumstance to its design.

324: A fawn-colored sea streaked here and there with tints of deepest orange.

325: There was a response, a half-breathless murmur of amazement and incredulity.

326: He sensed a helpless anger simmering in him.

327: He observed a manner nervously anxious to please.

328: His finely tuned senses told him a new trouble was dawning on his thickening mental horizon.

329: He/she sensed the person in front of him/her to be a nimble-witted opponent.

330: He/she sensed a pang of jealousy not unmingled with scorn.

331: From the outset, he thought the person a profound and rather irritating egotist by nature.

332: He watched as a quick shiver ruffled the brooding stillness of the water.

333: She sensed he held a secret sweeter than the sea or sky can whisper.

334: A sensation of golden sweetness and delight.

335: A sense of desolation and disillusionment overwhelmed her.

336: A sense of infinite peace brooded over the place.

337: A sense of repression was upon her.

338: A somber and breathless calm hung over the deepening eve.

339: She sensed a sort of eager, almost appealing amiability.

340: There followed a spacious sense of the amplitude of life's possibilities.

341: It was a stifling sensation of pain and suspense.

342: The sensation could be described as a sweet bewilderment of tremulous apprehension.

343: She drifted off in to a swiftly unrolling panorama of dreams.

344: It was a tumultuous rush of sensations.

345: He sensed a twinge of embarrassment.

346: She sensed a vast sweet silence creeping through the trees.

347: There was a sense of being absorbed in the scent and murmur of the night.

348: He sensed an acute note of distress in her voice.

349: He had the sense there was possibly an assumption of hostile intent.

350: She sensed an atmosphere thick with flattery and toadyism.

Part 9:
Tenacity

This section describes situations and examples of tenacity and focus or lack of it, taken from your character viewpoint, or that of others involved with or viewing the scene.

351: It was a laser-like focus.

352. He had the breaking strain of a hot Mars bar

353: He knew he would have to drive it like he stole it.

354: He held her passport in his hand; she held his manhood in hers.

355: He made a decision that defined him.

356: He would look for flaws in the Old Testament.

357: He didn't hold a grudge; he was just shy of telling people he forgave them.

358: He was like a Jack Russell with an old sock.

359: He was well aware that management of change could mean a change of management.

360: Nobody does, but somebody has to.

361: It was the only dead horse he knew who responded to flogging.

362: There is a line between good and evil. He held the line, he was the line.

363: Doing it my way will allow us to aggregate our personal gains.

364: He liked to train hard, fight easy.

365: You know you're brave because even though you may lose today, you will fight tomorrow.

366: Waylay destiny and bid him stand and deliver.

367: He was tenaciously untouched by the ruthless spirit of improvement.

368: He was a man of imperious will.

369: She was an antagonist worth her steel.

370: She had become hardened into convictions and resolves.

371: He drew near to a desperate resolve.

372: He threw a ton's weight of resolve upon his muscles.

373: His eyes shone with the pure fire of a great purpose.

374: His face lit with a fire of decision.

375: His soul was compressed into a single agony of prayer.

376: Seriousness lurked in the depths of her eyes.

377: She challenged his dissent.

378: She seemed the embodiment of dauntless resolution.

379: She stood her ground with the most perfect dignity.

380: The mystery obsessed him.
381: His tenacity was contained within the pith and sinew of mature manhood.
382: There was a strong assumption of superiority in the man.
383: He held a temper and tenacity which brooked no resistance.
384: He would take vengeance upon arrogant self-assertion.
385: The agonies of conscious failure would not stop him.
386: His tenacity was in the way that madness lays.
387: The blackest abyss of despair would be unable to overcome him.
388: The combined dictates of reason and experience would see him through.
389: His determination was the consequence of an agitated mind.
390: As he prepared himself, he knew the evil was irremediable.
391: The fitful swerving of passion finally did it.
392: The gratification of ambition kept him focused.
393: Such determination could be regarded as the handmaid of tyranny.
394: The innermost recesses of the human heart controlled her now.

395: Her tenacity would overcome the jostling and ugliness of life.

396: The long-delayed hour of retribution was gradually coming near.

397: The most exacting and exciting business would be carried out determinedly.

398: It was the outcome of unerring and dedicated observation.

399: It was provided by the overpowering force of circumstance and necessity.

400: The primitive instinct of self-preservation kicked in.

Part 10:
Time

Here are a few phrases and descriptions of 'time' as seen by a character or as seen in a particular and relative setting.

01: It was simply a fleeting moment in time.

402: He was a man, but was he a man of his time?

403: He hoped the time may come again.

404: In twenty years time you may call a nerd, Boss.

405: It was ever thus.

406: Tempus fugit (Time Fly's).

407: Time is a leash on the dog of an idea.

408: Since pussy was a cat.

409: Time is infinite, constant and unstoppable.

410: Time is nature's way of making sure everything doesn't happen at once.

410: Time stood still, but the world kept spinning.

411: Time, a dimension in which events can be ordered from the past, through the present into the future.

412: A time of disillusion followed the short conversation.

413: It was a confused and troublesome time.

414: It had the disenchanting effect of time and experience.

415: It had become the unbroken habit of a lifetime.

416: He felt that time was dissolving the circle of his friends.

417: They were plodding their way through times of unexampled difficulty.

418: These were well-concerted and well-timed stratagems.

419: The matter was suspended amid the direful calamities of the time.

429: His ideas would be borne onward by slow-footed time.

430: There were startling leaps over vast gulfs of time to contend with.

431: The hand of time was about to sweep them into oblivion.

432: The irresistible and ceaseless on-flow of time would affect the whole project.

433: He didn't need telling that the leaves of time drop stealthily.

434: It was a timely effusion of tearful sentiment.

435: The vast and shadowy stream of time would sweep all before it.

436: There was a time in his life where he might have trod the sunlit heights.

437: It appeared to her that time had passed unseen.

438: All the signs of the time indicated a necessity for change.

439: It would happen, but in the course of time.

440: He wanted to, but his allotted time was running away.

441: He was fairly sure that by this time it will be suspected.

442: Coming down to modern times would be an effort for him.

443: Was there time for all that might be said, he pondered?

444: He seems at times to be confused and at others be quite lucid in his delivery.

445: He felt inclined sometimes just to believe.

446: He knew he was trespassing too long on their time.

447: He hoped by this time they were all convinced.

448: She rather looked forward to a time when all would be behind her.

449: He regretted that time limited him.

450: He would waste no time in refuting the allegation.

Part 11:
Viewpoints

Everyone has a different view of a similar situation and this section provides a broad listing of views and viewpoints relating to people, situations and scenery.

451: He observed the Palladian portico heralding the entrance.

452: A Regency drawing room came in to view as they continued.

453: He thought he saw it to be a taut expression.

454: It was a view he was prepared for, deep in to the backroom sinews of war.

455: Others may not have thought so, but he was as well read as a magazine in a doctor's waiting room.

456: He knew without further movement it was the closest place to hell without getting burnt.

457: He was observed to be convalescing from open wallet surgery.

458: It was seen to be distilling the essence of female humanity.

459: He entered the room, dreading to be noticed, yet fearing to not be visible.

460: Gold as it appeared to him could only be described as the flesh of the sun god.

461: He appeared from a distance as the familiar stranger.

462: He generally dismissed any viewpoint when he had his beer goggles on.

463: He appeared to the casual observer to be so white he looked like a blood donor who couldn't say no.

464: His last date was so young she was seen arriving by skate board.

465: She surmised that from his look he wouldn't bite unless you asked nicely.

466: It was a viewpoint of being good from afar, but far from good.

467: He viewed it as being merely a grain of sand on a beach called America.

468: In his mind, he could see rocks jutting through rolling waves of sand.

469: It was the sight of a sun that simply melts over the horizon.

470: He viewed the meager traffic passing by.

471: From his viewpoint, the whole situation had become vanishingly small.

472: He closed his eyes and pondered upon the things you see when you haven't got a gun.

473: He viewed the whole matter through a

prism of new understanding.

474: His view appeared to be corrected by willful blindness.

475: From a period of close observation, he seemed to know the cost of everything and the value of nothing.

476: He needed to question his taking if a slightly one-sided point of view.

477: His views are about to be altered in many respects.

478: It seemed he was about to take a pessimistic view of things.

479: He noticed it had become a campaign of unbridled ferocity.

480: He gave out a deep authentic impression of disinterestedness.

481: He projected a view to others as being a figure full of decision and dignity.

482: She noticed a flame of scarlet creeping in a swift diagonal across his cheeks.

482: He saw in her eyes the glassy expression of inattention.

483: As he watched from a distance, he noticed a gusty breeze blew her hair about unheeded.

484: He saw it only as a portent full of possible danger.

485: He looked up to observe a propitious sky, marbled with pearly white.

486: A quick flame leapt in his eyes but went unnoticed.

487: As he watched he observed a shimmer of golden sun shaking through the trees.

488: She noted the sigh of large contentment.

489: She absorbed the near perfect silence except for a soundless breeze that was little more than a whisper.

490: It appeared at first to be a strange compound of contradictory elements.

491: It was presented as a super-refinement of taste.

492: He spoke to her in a tone of arduous admiration.

493: An unobserved wind had strayed through the gardens.

494: As she entered the room, all the lesser lights paled into insignificance.

495: All he was left with was a vague jumble of chaotic impressions.

496: He noticed the woman across the room from him had an eager and thirsty ear.

497: It was seen by most as an expression of rare and inexplicable personal energy.

498: His view changed as he suddenly came across an impenetrable screen of foliage.

499: He noticed the long suffering father appealing to the urgent temper of youth.

500: The passenger looked distressed as the long train swept away into the golden distance.

501: He observed the complete scene with bookish precision and professional peculiarity.

THE END

www.quentincope.co.uk

MECURIAN BOOKS

https://mecurianbooks.com